THE WEIGHT WATCHERS COOKBOOK 2025

Simple and delicious recipes for sustainable weight loss without compromising flavor. Includes vegan options, diabetes-friendly and air fryer dishes.

EDYTH BREESE

Copyright © [Edyth Breese] 2024

All rights reserved. No part of this book may be reproduced or transmitted in any form or by any means, electronic or mechanical, including photocopying, recording, or by any information storage and retrieval system, without written permission from the copyright holder.

DISCLAIMER

The information provided in "The Weight watchers Cookbook 2025" is for general informational purposes only. While every effort has been made to ensure accuracy and completeness, the author/publisher assumes no responsibility for errors, inaccuracies, or omissions. Individuals using the recipes or advice contained in this cookbook are responsible for their own health and well-being. Consult with a healthcare professional or nutritionist for personalized guidance. The author/publisher disclaims any liability for damages or injuries resulting from the use of the information presented in this cookbook.

THANK YOU FOR CHOOSING THIS BOOK

Dear Valued Reader,

From the bottom of my heart, I want to express my deepest gratitude to you for purchasing **The Weight Watchers Cookbook 2025.** Your decision to invest in this book is a testament to your commitment to health, wellness, and a better you.

It's my sincere hope that every recipe, tip, and piece of advice within these pages empowers you to take charge of your weight loss journey with confidence and joy. Whether you're just starting out or looking for fresh inspiration, I'm honored to be part of your path toward success.

Remember, you are not alone on this journey. Every small win matters. Celebrate your progress, be kind to yourself, and know that each healthy choice you make is a step closer to your goals. Your health is your wealth, and you deserve every bit of it.

With heartfelt gratitude and encouragement,

Edyth Breese.

This cookbook belongs to:

_____

_____

_____

ABOUT THE AUTHOR

Edyth Breese is a devoted chef and nutrition expert who ardently advocates for healthful living by crafting savory, nutrient-rich meals. Her culinary path is distinguished by innovation and a deep grasp of dietary principles, allowing her to merge her enthusiasm for gastronomy with a commitment to health promotion. In her role as a chef, Edyth demonstrates a broad expertise in various global cuisines, consistently emphasizing the preparation of dishes that satisfy the palate while enhancing health. Her inventive culinary style showcases her insight into the intricate interplay of taste and health benefits.

As a nutritionist, Edyth has cultivated a greater respect for the impact of conscious food choices. Her approach is grounded in the belief that feeding the body involves more than simply monitoring caloric intake; it's about making knowledgeable, enjoyable decisions that pave the way for a lasting, healthful way of life.

TABLE OF CONTENTS

INTRODUCTION 7
- Why this book will change the way you see weight loss 8
- My Personal Message to You 9
- 5 Key Messages to Remember 9

CHAPTER 1: ALL ABOUT WEIGHT WATCHERS 11
- The Science Behind the Weight Watchers Program 11
- How to Set SMART Goals 13

CHAPTER 2: BREAKFAST 15
- Banana Oat Pancakes 16
- Veggie Egg Muffins 17
- Greek Yogurt Berry Parfait 18
- Spinach and Mushroom Omelette 19
- Overnight Chia Pudding 20
- Avocado Toast with Egg 21
- Peanut Butter Banana Smoothie . 22
- Cottage Cheese & Berry Bowl 23
- Sweet Potato Breakfast Hash 24
- Apple Cinnamon Oatmeal 25

CHAPTER 3: LUNCH 27
- Grilled Chicken and Quinoa Bowl 28
- Turkey & Hummus Wrap 29
- Veggie Stuffed Bell Peppers 30
- Zucchini Noodles with Shrimp 31
- Chickpea Avocado Salad 32
- Spaghetti Squash with Marinara . 33
- Grilled Turkey Burger 34
- Black Bean & Corn Quesadilla 35
- Lemon Garlic Salmon with Asparagus 36
- Chicken Caesar Lettuce Wraps 37

CHAPTER 4: DINNER 39
- Garlic Butter Shrimp Zoodles 40
- Lemon Herb Baked Chicken Breast 41
- Beef and Broccoli Stir Fry 42
- Turkey Meatball Marinara 43
- Creamy Mushroom Chicken 44
- Teriyaki Salmon Bowls 45
- Honey Garlic Glazed Pork Chops. 46
- Vegetable Fried Rice 47
- Spinach and Feta Stuffed Chicken Breast 48

CHAPTER 5: VEGAN RECIPES 49
- Chickpea and Spinach Curry 50
- Tofu and Vegetable Stir-Fry 51
- Vegan Lentil Tacos 52
- Sweet Potato and Black Bean Chili 53
- Vegan Mushroom Stroganoff 54
- Vegan Buddha Bowl 55
- Vegan BBQ Jackfruit Sandwich ... 56

CHAPTER 6: DIABETES FRIENDLY RECIPES 57

Turkey and Zucchini Meatballs ... 58

Baked Chicken with Roasted Brussels Sprouts 59

Black Bean and Quinoa Stuffed Bell Peppers 60

Lemon Garlic Roasted Cauliflower 61

Eggplant Stir-Fry 62

Vegetable and Chickpea Soup 63

CHAPTER 7: SMOOTHIES 65

Strawberry Banana Bliss Smoothie 66

Tropical Green Detox Smoothie ... 67

Blueberry Almond Power Smoothie 68

Chocolate Peanut Butter Protein Smoothie 69

Mango Coconut Smoothie 70

Creamy Avocado Berry Smoothie 71

Cinnamon Roll Smoothie 72

Carrot Cake Smoothie 73

Orange Creamsicle Smoothie 74

Apple Pie Smoothie 75

CHAPTER 8: AIR FRYER RECIPES 77

Crispy Air Fryer Chicken Tenders 78

Air Fryer Garlic Parmesan Zucchini Fries 79

Air Fryer Turkey Meatballs 80

Air Fryer Buffalo Cauliflower Bites 81

Air Fryer Crispy Tofu Bites 82

Air Fryer Sweet Potato Fries 83

Air Fryer Garlic Shrimp 84

Air Fryer Crispy Chickpeas 85

Air Fryer Spiced Apple Chips 86

CHAPTER 9: SOUPS AND STEWS 87

Classic Vegetable Soup 88

Hearty Lentil Stew 89

Chicken Tortilla Soup 90

Creamy Cauliflower Soup 91

Beef and Barley Stew 92

Italian Minestrone Soup 93

Butternut Squash Soup 94

CONCLUSION 95

5 WEEKS MEAL PLANNER 97

BONUS GIFT FOR YOU 102

INTRODUCTION

I still remember the exact moment I realized something had to change. It wasn't during a doctor's visit or after stepping on the scale. It was while trying to button up a pair of jeans I'd worn for years. No matter how much I pulled, twisted, or sucked in my stomach, that stubborn button wasn't budging. Frustration washed over me, followed by a flood of self-doubt. I'd been "watching my weight" for what felt like forever, but clearly, I'd been watching it go in the wrong direction.

That's when I stumbled upon Weight Watchers. At first, I'll admit, I was skeptical. "Another diet program?" I thought. I'd tried so many approaches before—cutting carbs, counting calories, and eating nothing but cabbage soup for a week (never again!). But Weight Watchers felt different. There was no "eat this, not that" ultimatum. Instead, I learned about balance, flexibility, and how to make better choices without sacrificing my favorite foods. It wasn't just a diet; it was a lifestyle change. I'm not going to say it was easy at first, but it was sustainable—and that's what made all the difference.

This book, The Weight Watchers Cookbook 2025, was born out of that journey. It's a culmination of everything I've learned, experienced, and wish I'd known from the start. I've poured my heart into creating something that's more than a collection of recipes. It's a resource, a guide, and, I hope, a source of inspiration for you.

This isn't just another cookbook. It's your guide, your coach, and your cheerleader all in one. The Weight Watchers Cookbook 2025 was created with you in mind. Regardless of whether you're new to Weight Watchers or a seasoned pro looking for fresh inspiration, this book will meet you where you are. You'll learn how to start, stay consistent, and succeed on the Weight Watchers program. More importantly, you'll discover how to make this a lifestyle you love, not a punishment you endure.

Let's be real, weight loss isn't always easy, and I won't tell you it is. But here's the good news: you don't have to do it alone. This book is here to guide you, every step of the way. No gimmicks. No starvation. Just real, flavorful food that works for real, everyday life.

Why this book will change the way you see weight loss

If you've ever felt overwhelmed by weight loss programs, I want to make this as simple as possible. Weight Watchers isn't about restriction — it's about freedom. Freedom to enjoy your favorite foods (yes, even dessert), freedom from guilt, and freedom to live life fully.

Here's what you'll find in this book:

- ➢ Delicious, Easy Recipes: From comforting breakfasts to family-friendly dinners, you'll never run out of ideas.
- ➢ Meal Planning Made Simple: No more guessing what's for dinner. Learn how to plan ahead and save time.
- ➢ Smart Swaps & Healthy Hacks: Small changes can lead to big results. You'll learn easy ways to make your favorite meals healthier.

- Diabetes-Friendly Recipes: Blood sugar-friendly meals that don't sacrifice taste.
- Motivation & Support: This book is designed to keep you inspired, even on the tough days.

This book is designed to be your ultimate guide, covering every stage of your journey — from the first step to the finish line (and beyond). It's here to remind you that you're stronger, smarter, and more capable than you think.

My Personal Message to You

If there's one thing I want you to know as you start this journey, it's this: You are enough, right now, just as you are. Losing weight doesn't make you "better" or "more worthy." Your worth isn't tied to a number on a scale. But if you're ready to feel healthier, more energetic, and more confident, I'm here to help you get there.

Some days will be easy, and others will feel like an uphill climb. And that's okay. Progress isn't about perfection — it's about persistence. If you slip up, you don't have to "start over." You just keep going. Every meal is a new opportunity to make a choice that serves you. I know you can do this. You're here, reading this book, which means you've already taken the first step. You're ready.

5 Key Messages to Remember

I want you to walk away with these 5 truths in your heart:

- You Are Not Alone — Weight loss is hard, but you don't have to face it alone. This book is your guide, and I'm here for you every step of the way.
- Small Steps Lead to Big Wins — You don't have to change everything overnight. Small changes add up to life-changing results.

- Progress, Not Perfection — This isn't about being perfect every day. It's about showing up for yourself, even when it's hard. You Deserve to Feel Good — This isn't punishment. It's about feeling strong, energetic, and in control of your health.
- Every Meal is a New Chance — No matter how "off track" you feel, every meal is a fresh start. Keep going. You've got this.

CHAPTER 1: ALL ABOUT WEIGHT WATCHERS

The Science Behind the Weight Watchers Program

Weight Watchers isn't about guesswork. It's based on research-backed principles that focus on **nutrition, behavior change, and long-term habit-building**. Unlike restrictive "quick-fix" diets, this approach is rooted in sustainability, flexibility, and a deep understanding of how the human mind and body respond to food, hunger, and satisfaction.

If you've ever felt like weight loss is impossible to sustain, the problem wasn't *you*—it was the system you were following. But with Weight Watchers, you're working *with* your body, not against it.

So, what makes it work so well? Let's break down the key pillars of the program.

1. The Power of the Points System

At the heart of Weight Watchers is its revolutionary **Points System**. Instead of counting calories (which can feel tedious), Weight Watchers assigns foods a "Smart Points" value. These points are calculated based on more than just calories. They factor in:

- **Calories** — Foods with more calories have higher Points.

- **Saturated Fat** — Unhealthy fats raise the Points value, encouraging you to opt for healthier fats.

- **Sugar** — Foods high in sugar get higher Points because of their low nutritional value.

- **Protein** — Foods high in protein often have *lower* Points because protein helps you feel fuller longer.

This system nudges you toward smarter choices by encouraging whole, nutrient-dense foods (like fruits, veggies, and lean proteins) and discouraging processed, sugar-laden items. But here's the twist: **No food is off-limits.** If you want a cookie, you can have one, you just have to "spend" your Points wisely.

---

2. Zero Point Foods: Your Secret Weapon

If you've ever tried a traditional diet, you know that hunger can be a major roadblock. That's why Weight Watchers created **Zero Point Foods** — a list of over 200+ foods that you can eat without tracking or counting.

These foods include:

- Fruits (like apples, berries, bananas, and oranges)
- Vegetables (like spinach, broccoli, carrots, and tomatoes)
- Lean proteins (like chicken breast, tofu, beans, and eggs)

The logic behind Zero Point Foods is simple:

- **These foods are hard to overeat.** When was the last time you "binged" on broccoli?
- **They're filling and nutrient-dense.** They help you feel satisfied, reducing the urge to snack on high-Point foods.
- **They encourage healthier eating patterns.** By making whole, unprocessed foods more accessible, you naturally make better choices.

---

3. The Role of Satiety and Fullness

You know that "bottomless pit" feeling when you're starving? It's hard to make good choices when you're that hungry. Weight Watchers understands this, which is why they emphasize foods that promote *satiety* (the feeling of fullness).

Here's how it works:

- **Protein + Fiber = Fullness** — High-protein foods (like chicken, beans, and eggs) keep you full for longer, and fiber (found in fruits, veggies, and whole grains) slows down digestion.

- **Eat More, Not Less** — Many low-Point foods (like vegetables) are naturally large in volume but low in calories. For example, a large plate of roasted vegetables might have the same calories as a small slice of cake, but the veggies will keep you fuller longer.

---

5. The Power of Flexibility and Customization

Unlike rigid diets that demand "Eat this, not that," Weight Watchers allows you to personalize your approach. Your daily Points allowance is tailored to your unique goals, height, weight, and age.

This approach allows for:

- **Custom Points Budgets** — If you're taller, more active, or have different goals, you'll get more Points than someone with a smaller frame or less active lifestyle.

- **Weekly "Flex" Points** — In addition to your daily Points, you get a "weekly Points bank" that you can use for special occasions, like a night out or a holiday.

How to Set SMART Goals

To set realistic goals, you need to think S.M.A.R.T. — Specific, Measurable, Achievable, Relevant, and Time-bound. Here's what that looks like:

- Specific: "I want to lose weight" becomes "I want to lose 10 pounds."
- Measurable: Track progress with scales, clothing fit, or how you feel.

- Achievable: Losing 10 pounds in 3 months is achievable. Losing 10 pounds in a week is not.
- Relevant: Your goal should align with your larger health goals.
- Time-bound: Put a deadline on it. Instead of "someday," set a date.

Focus on Non-Scale Victories (NSVs)

It's easy to obsess over the number on the scale, but weight isn't the only way to measure progress. Here are a few other signs you're on the right track:

- Your clothes fit better.
- You have more energy.
- Your cravings have decreased.
- You feel more confident and in control.

CHAPTER 2: BREAKFAST

BANANA OAT PANCAKES

Smart Points: 4 | Servings: 2 | Prep Time: 5 min | Cook Time: 10 min

Ingredients

- 1 medium ripe banana (mashed)
- 1/2 cup rolled oats
- 1/4 cup unsweetened almond milk
- 1 large egg
- 1/2 tsp baking powder
- 1/2 tsp vanilla extract
- 1/2 tsp ground cinnamon
- Cooking spray

Instructions

1. In a bowl, mash the banana until smooth. Add oats, almond milk, egg, baking powder, vanilla, and cinnamon. Mix until combined.

2. Heat a non-stick pan over medium heat and coat with cooking spray.

3. Pour 1/4 cup of the batter onto the pan for each pancake. Cook for 2-3 minutes per side or until golden brown.

4. Serve with fresh fruit or a drizzle of honey (optional).

Nutritional Info (per serving)

Calories: 180 | Protein: 6g | Carbs: 30g | Fat: 4g | Fiber

VEGGIE EGG MUFFINS

Smart Points: 2 | Servings: 6 | Prep Time: 10 min | Cook Time: 20 min

Ingredients

- 6 large eggs
- 1/2 cup spinach (chopped)
- 1/4 cup diced red bell pepper
- 1/4 cup diced onion
- 1/4 cup low-fat shredded cheese
- 1/4 cup mushrooms (chopped)
- Salt & pepper to taste
- Cooking spray

Instructions

1. Preheat oven to 375°F (190°C) and spray a 12-cup muffin tin with cooking spray.

2. In a large bowl, whisk the eggs. Add spinach, bell pepper, onion, mushrooms, cheese, salt, and pepper. Stir well.

3. Pour the mixture into each muffin cup, filling 3/4 of the way.

4. Bake for 20 minutes or until eggs are set. Let cool slightly before removing from the pan.

Nutritional Info (per serving)

Calories: 85 | Protein: 7g | Carbs: 2| Fat: 5g | Fiber:

GREEK YOGURT BERRY PARFAIT

Smart Points: 3 | Servings: 1 | Prep Time: 5 min | Cook Time: 0 min

Ingredients

- 1/2 cup non-fat Greek yogurt
- 1/4 cup mixed berries (strawberries, blueberries, raspberries)
- 1 tbsp granola (low-sugar)
- 1/2 tsp chia seeds
- 1 tsp honey (optional)

Instructions

1. In a glass or jar, layer Greek yogurt, berries, granola, and chia seeds.

2. Drizzle honey on top, if using.

3. Enjoy immediately or refrigerate for later.

Nutritional Info (per serving)

Calories: 150 | **Protein:** 9g | **Carbs:** 20g | **Fat:** 3g | **Fiber:** 3g

SPINACH AND MUSHROOM OMELETTE

Smart Points: 2 | Servings: 1 | Prep Time: 5 min | Cook Time: 5 min

Ingredients

- 2 large eggs
- 1/4 cup spinach (chopped)
- 1/4 cup mushrooms (chopped)
- 1 tbsp low-fat shredded cheese
- 1/4 tsp garlic powder
- Salt & pepper to taste
- Cooking spray

Instructions

1. In a bowl, whisk eggs, garlic powder, salt, and pepper.

2. Spray a non-stick pan with cooking spray and sauté mushrooms and spinach until soft.

3. Pour in the egg mixture and cook for 2-3 minutes, then fold the omelette in half.

4. Sprinkle cheese on top and serve hot.

Nutritional Info (per serving)

Calories: 160 | Protein: 12g | Carbs: 3g | Fat: 11g | Fiber: 1

OVERNIGHT CHIA PUDDING

Smart Points: 4 | Servings: 2 | Prep Time: 5 min | Cook Time: 0 min

Ingredients

- 2 tbsp chia seeds
- 1/2 cup unsweetened almond milk
- 1/4 tsp vanilla extract
- 1/4 cup mixed berries (for topping)

Instructions

1. In a jar, mix chia seeds, almond milk, and vanilla.

2. Cover and refrigerate overnight (or at least 4 hours).

3. Top with berries before serving.

Nutritional Info (per serving)

Calories: 120 | Protein: 3g | Carbs: 10g | Fat: 7g | Fiber: 6g

Avocado Toast with Egg

Smart Points: 5 | Servings: 1 | Prep Time: 5 min | Cook Time: 5 min

Ingredients

- 1 slice whole-grain bread
- 1/4 avocado (mashed)
- 1 large egg (fried or poached)
- Salt, pepper, and red pepper flakes (optional)

Instructions

1. Toast the bread and spread mashed avocado on top.

2. Top with a cooked egg and sprinkle with salt, pepper, and red pepper flakes.

Nutritional Info (per serving)

Calories: 210 | Protein: 9g | Carbs: 20g | Fat: 12g | Fiber: 6g

PEANUT BUTTER BANANA SMOOTHIE

Smart Points: 5 | Servings: 1 | Prep Time: 5 min | Cook Time: 0 min

Ingredients

- 1 medium banana
- 1 tbsp natural peanut butter
- 1/2 cup unsweetened almond milk
- 1/4 cup non-fat Greek yogurt
- 1/2 cup ice cubes

Instructions

1. Blend all ingredients until smooth.
2. Pour into a glass and enjoy.

Nutritional Info (per serving)

Calories: 230 | Protein: 8g | Carbs: 35g | Fat: 8g | Fiber: 4g

COTTAGE CHEESE & BERRY BOWL

Smart Points: 3 | Servings: 1 | Prep Time: 5 min | Cook Time: 0 min

Ingredients

- 1/2 cup low-fat cottage cheese
- 1/4 cup mixed berries
- 1/2 tsp chia seeds

Instructions

1. In a bowl, combine cottage cheese, berries, and chia seeds.
2. Serve fresh.

Nutritional Info (per serving)

Calories: 120 | Protein: 10g | Carbs: 8g | Fat: 4g | Fiber: 2g

SWEET POTATO BREAKFAST HASH

Smart Points: 5 | Servings: 2 | Prep Time: 10 min | Cook Time: 20 min

Ingredients

- 1 medium sweet potato (diced)
- 1/4 onion (diced)
- 1/4 red bell pepper (diced)
- 2 large eggs
- Cooking spray

Instructions

1. Cook sweet potatoes in a skillet until soft. Add onion and pepper, sauté for 5 minutes.

2. Make 2 wells in the hash and crack an egg into each well.

3. Cover the skillet and cook until eggs are set.

Nutritional Info (per serving)

Calories: 200 | Protein: 9g | Carbs: 28g | Fat: 6g | Fiber: 4g

APPLE CINNAMON OATMEAL

Smart Points: 4 | Servings: 1 | Prep Time: 5 min | Cook Time: 5 min

Ingredients

- 1/2 cup rolled oats
- 1/2 cup unsweetened almond milk
- 1/2 apple (chopped)
- 1/2 tsp cinnamon

Instructions

1. Cook oats, almond milk, and apple in a pot for 5 minutes.

2. Sprinkle with cinnamon before serving.

Nutritional Info

Calories: 190 | Protein: 5g | Carbs: 38g | Fiber: 5g

CHAPTER 3: LUNCH

GRILLED CHICKEN AND QUINOA BOWL

Smart Points: 6 | Servings: 2 | Prep Time: 10 min | Cook Time: 20 min

Ingredients

- 1/2 cup cooked quinoa
- 1 small boneless, skinless chicken breast (about 4 oz)
- 1/4 cup chopped cucumber
- 1/4 cup cherry tomatoes (halved)
- 1/4 cup diced red onion
- 1/4 cup crumbled feta cheese
- 1 tbsp olive oil
- 1/2 lemon (juiced)
- 1/2 tsp garlic powder
- Salt and pepper (to taste)

Instructions

1. Cook quinoa according to package instructions and set aside.

2. Season chicken with salt, pepper, and garlic powder. Grill for 4-5 minutes on each side or until fully cooked. Slice the chicken into strips.

3. In a bowl, combine quinoa, cucumber, tomatoes, red onion, and feta cheese.

4. Top with grilled chicken. Drizzle olive oil and lemon juice on top. Toss to combine and serve.

Nutritional Info (per serving)

Calories: 320 | Protein: 28g | Carbs: 25g | Fat: 11g | Fiber: 3g

TURKEY & HUMMUS WRAP

Smart Points: 5 | Servings: 1 | Prep Time: 5 min | Cook Time: 0 min

Ingredients

- 1 whole-wheat tortilla
- 2 oz sliced turkey breast (low-sodium)
- 2 tbsp hummus
- 1/4 cup shredded carrots
- 1/4 cup baby spinach
- 2 slices cucumber

Instructions

Spread hummus on the tortilla.

Layer turkey, carrots, spinach, and cucumber.

Roll the tortilla tightly and slice in half. Serve fresh.

Nutritional Info (per serving)

Calories: 280 | Protein: 22g | Carbs: 30g | Fat: 8g | Fiber: 5g

VEGGIE STUFFED BELL PEPPERS

Smart Points: 4 | Servings: 2 | Prep Time: 10 min | Cook Time: 25 min

Ingredients

- 2 large bell peppers (halved, seeds removed
- 1/2 cup cooked brown rice
- 1/2 cup black beans (cooked)
- 1/4 cup diced tomatoes
- 1/4 cup corn (fresh or frozen)
- 1/4 cup shredded low-fat cheese
- 1/2 tsp chili powder
- 1/4 tsp cumin
- Salt and pepper (to taste)

Instructions

1. Preheat oven to 375°F (190°C).

2. Mix rice, black beans, tomatoes, corn, chili powder, cumin, salt, and pepper in a bowl.

3. Stuff each bell pepper half with the rice mixture.

4. Place on a baking sheet and bake for 20 minutes. Add cheese on top and bake for another 5 minutes.

Nutritional Info (per serving)

Calories: 250 | Protein: 10g | Carbs: 40g | Fat: 4g | Fiber: 9g

ZUCCHINI NOODLES WITH SHRIMP

Smart Points: 3 | Servings: 2 | Prep Time: 10 min | Cook Time: 10 min

Ingredients

- 2 medium zucchinis (spiralized)
- 6 oz shrimp (peeled and deveined)
- 1 tbsp olive oil
- 2 garlic cloves (minced)
- 1/4 cup cherry tomatoes (halved)
- Salt, pepper, and red pepper flakes (to taste)

Instructions

1. Heat olive oil in a pan over medium heat. Add garlic and cook for 1 minute.

2. Add shrimp, season with salt, pepper, and red pepper flakes. Cook for 3-4 minutes per side.

3. Add zucchini noodles and tomatoes. Toss for 2-3 minutes. Serve hot.

Nutritional Info (per serving)

Calories: 200 | Protein: 24g | Carbs: 8g | Fat: 8g | Fiber: 2g

CHICKPEA AVOCADO SALAD

Smart Points: 5 | Servings: 2 | Prep Time: 10 min | Cook Time: 0 min

Ingredients

- 1/2 cup canned chickpeas (rinsed and drained)
- 1/2 avocado (chopped)
- 1/4 cup chopped cucumber
- 1/4 cup diced red onion
- 1/2 lemon (juiced)
- 1 tbsp olive oil
- Salt and pepper (to taste)

Instructions

1. In a bowl, combine chickpeas, avocado, cucumber, and red onion.

2. Drizzle with olive oil and lemon juice. Toss and season with salt and pepper.

Nutritional Info (per serving)

Calories: 250 | Protein: 6g | Carbs: 22g | Fat: 15g | Fiber: 8g

SPAGHETTI SQUASH WITH MARINARA

Smart Points: 4 | Servings: 2 | Prep Time: 10 min | Cook Time: 30 min

Ingredients

- 1 medium spaghetti squash
- 1/2 cup marinara sauce (low sugar)
- 1/4 cup shredded parmesan cheese
- Salt, pepper, and garlic powder (to taste)

Instructions

1. Cut squash in half, remove seeds, and bake at 375°F (190°C) for 30 minutes.

2. Scrape squash into "noodles" using a fork.

3. Top with marinara sauce and parmesan cheese.

Nutritional Info (per serving)

Calories: 200 | Protein: 9g | Carbs: 30g | Fat: 5g | Fiber: 6g

GRILLED TURKEY BURGER

Smart Points: 5 | Servings: 2 | Prep Time: 10 min | Cook Time: 15 min

Ingredients

- 1/2 lb ground turkey (93% lean)
- 1/4 cup chopped onion
- 1 garlic clove (minced)
- Salt and pepper (to taste)
- 2 whole-grain buns
- Lettuce, tomato, and onion (for topping)

Instructions

1. Mix ground turkey, onion, garlic, salt, and pepper. Shape into 2 patties.

2. Grill for 6-7 minutes per side. Serve on buns with toppings.

Nutritional Info (per serving)

Calories: 320 | Protein: 28g | Carbs: 32g | Fat: 8g | Fiber: 6g

BLACK BEAN & CORN QUESADILLA

Smart Points: 7 | Servings: 2 | Prep Time: 5 min | Cook Time: 10 min

Ingredients

- 2 whole-wheat tortillas
- 1/2 cup black beans (cooked)
- 1/4 cup corn (fresh or frozen)
- 1/4 cup shredded cheese
- Cooking spray

Instructions

1. Heat tortilla in a pan. Add beans, corn, and cheese.

2. Top with another tortilla and cook for 3-4 minutes on each side. Slice into wedges.

Nutritional Info (per serving)

Calories: 350 | Protein: 15g | Carbs: 50g | Fat: 8g | Fiber: 10g

LEMON GARLIC SALMON WITH ASPARAGUS

Smart Points: 5 | Servings: 2 | Prep Time: 10 min | Cook Time: 15 min

Ingredients

- 2 (4 oz) salmon fillets
- 1/2 lb fresh asparagus (trimmed)
- 1 tbsp olive oil
- 2 garlic cloves (minced)
- 1/2 lemon (juiced)
- Salt and black pepper (to taste)
- 1/4 tsp red pepper flakes (optional)

Instructions

1. Preheat oven to 400°F (200°C).

2. Line a baking sheet with parchment paper. Place the salmon fillets and asparagus on the sheet.

3. Drizzle olive oil, lemon juice, minced garlic, salt, pepper, and red pepper flakes over the salmon and asparagus.

4. Bake for 12-15 minutes, or until the salmon is cooked through and flakes easily with a fork.

5. Serve hot with a lemon wedge on the side.

Nutritional Info (per serving)

Calories: 290 | Protein: 27g | Carbs: 6g | Fat: 17g | Fiber: 2g

CHICKEN CAESAR LETTUCE WRAPS

Smart Points: 4 | Servings: 2 | Prep Time: 10 min | Cook Time: 0 min

Ingredients

- 1 cup cooked, shredded chicken breast (skinless)
- 4 large romaine lettuce leaves
- 1/4 cup low-fat Caesar dressing
- 1/4 cup grated parmesan cheese
- 1/4 cup cherry tomatoes (halved)
- 1/4 cup croutons (optional for crunch, but will increase Smart Points)
- Black pepper (to taste)

Instructions

1. In a bowl, mix shredded chicken, Caesar dressing, and black pepper.

2. Lay out the romaine lettuce leaves and divide the chicken mixture among them.

3. Top with parmesan cheese, cherry tomatoes, and croutons (if using).

Serve fresh and enjoy.

Nutritional Info (per serving)

Calories: 250 | Protein: 30g | Carbs: 8g | Fat: 10g | Fiber: 2g

LOVE ZERO POINT FOODS?

CHECK OUT MY PREVIOUS BOOK!

If you've been enjoying the recipes and tips in *The Weight Watchers Cookbook 2025,* you'll absolutely love my previous book, **Quick and Easy Zero Point Weight Loss Cookbook.** This book is packed with flavorful, satisfying recipes made entirely from Zero Point foods inspired by the Weight Watchers approach, to help you stay on track with your weight loss goals without the need to count or track points. It is perfect for busy days when you need simple, hassle-free meals and full of nutritious ingredients that won't break the bank.

Simply scan the QR code below to explore the book instantly:

CHAPTER 4: DINNER

GARLIC BUTTER SHRIMP ZOODLES

Smart Points: | Servings: 2 | Prep Time: 10 min | Cook Time: 10 min

Ingredients

- 2 medium zucchinis (spiralized)
- 8oz shrimp (peeled and deveined)
- 2 tsp unsalted butter
- 2 garlic cloves (minced)
- 1 tbsp olive oil
- 1/4 tsp red chili flakes (optional)
- Salt and black pepper (to taste)
- 1 tbsp chopped fresh parsley (for garnish)

Instructions

1. Heat olive oil in a pan over medium heat. Add garlic and cook for 1 minute.

2. Add shrimp and season with salt, pepper, and chili flakes. Cook for 2-3 minutes per side.

3. Add butter and spiralized zucchini. Toss to combine for 2-3 minutes.

4. Serve warm, garnished with fresh parsley.

Nutritional Info (per serving)

Calories: 240 | Protein: 28g | Carbs: 8g | Fat: 10g | Fiber: 2g

LEMON HERB BAKED CHICKEN BREAST

Smart Points: 3 | Servings: 4 | Prep Time: 10 min | Cook Time: 25 min

Ingredients

- 4 (4 oz) boneless, skinless chicken breasts
- 2 tbsp olive oil
- 1/2 lemon (juiced)
- 2 garlic cloves (minced)
- 1 tsp dried oregano
- 1 tsp dried thyme
- 1/2 tsp salt
- 1/4 tsp black pepper

Instructions

1. Preheat oven to 400°F (200°C).

2. In a small bowl, mix olive oil, lemon juice, garlic, oregano, thyme, salt, and pepper.

3. Coat chicken breasts with the marinade and place on a baking sheet.

4. Bake for 20-25 minutes or until the internal temperature reaches 165°F (74°C).

Nutritional Info (per serving)

Calories: 210 | Protein: 30g | Carbs: 2g | Fat: 9g | Fiber: 0g

BEEF AND BROCCOLI STIR FRY

Smart Points: 5 | Servings: 2 | Prep Time: 10 min | Cook Time: 15 min

Ingredients

- 6 oz lean beef (sliced)
- 2 cups broccoli florets
- 2 garlic cloves (minced)
- 1 tbsp olive oil
- 2 tbsp low-sodium soy sauce
- 1 tbsp cornstarch
- 1/2 cup beef broth
- Salt and pepper (to taste)

Instructions

1. Heat oil in a pan. Sauté garlic for 1 minute.

2. Add beef and cook for 3-4 minutes. Remove from pan.

3. Add broccoli and sauté for 2 minutes.

4. In a bowl, mix soy sauce, cornstarch, and beef broth. Pour into pan and simmer.

5. Return beef to pan and cook for 3 minutes.

Nutritional Info (per serving)

Calories: 320 | Protein: 28g | Carbs: 12g | Fat: 16g | Fiber: 4g

TURKEY MEATBALL MARINARA

Smart Points: 6 | Servings: 4 | Prep Time: 10 min | Cook Time: 25 min

Ingredients

- 1/2 lb ground turkey (93% lean)
- 1/4 cup breadcrumbs
- 1 egg (lightly beaten)
- 2 garlic cloves (minced)
- 1/2 tsp Italian seasoning
- Salt and pepper (to taste)
- 1 cup marinara sauce (low-sugar)

Instructions

1. Preheat oven to 375°F (190°C).

2. Mix ground turkey, breadcrumbs, egg, garlic, Italian seasoning, salt, and pepper.

3. Shape mixture into 12 small meatballs. Bake for 20 minutes.

4. Heat marinara sauce in a pan. Add baked meatballs and simmer for 5 minutes.

Nutritional Info (per serving)

Calories: 290 | Protein: 30g | Carbs: 18g | Fat: 10g | Fiber: 3g

CREAMY MUSHROOM CHICKEN

Smart Points: 5 | Servings: 2 | Prep Time: 10 min | Cook Time: 20 min

Ingredients

- 2 boneless, skinless chicken breasts
- 1 cup mushrooms (sliced)
- 2 garlic cloves (minced)
- 1/4 cup unsweetened almond milk
- 1/4 cup chicken broth
- 1 tbsp olive oil
- 1 tbsp cornstarch

Instructions

1. Cook chicken in olive oil for 5-6 minutes per side. Remove from pan.

2. Sauté mushrooms and garlic for 3 minutes.

3. Mix almond milk, chicken broth, and cornstarch. Add to pan and stir until thickened.

4. Return chicken to pan and cook for 5 minutes.

Nutritional Info (per serving)

Calories: 280 | Protein: 32g | Carbs: 10g | Fat: 10g | Fiber: 2g

TERIYAKI SALMON BOWLS

Smart Points: 7 | Servings: 2 | Prep Time: 10 min | Cook Time: 20 min

Ingredient

- 2 (4 oz) salmon fillets
- 1/2 cup brown rice (cooked)
- 1/4 cup teriyaki sauce
- 1/2 cup steamed broccoli

Instructions

1. Bake salmon at 375°F (190°C) for 15 minutes.

2. Brush with teriyaki sauce and cook for another 5 minutes.

3. Serve with brown rice and steamed broccoli.

Nutritional Info (per serving)

Calories: 340 | Protein: 28g | Carbs: 30g | Fat: 10g | Fiber: 4g

HONEY GARLIC GLAZED PORK CHOPS

Smart Points: 6 | Servings: 2 | Prep Time: 10 min | Cook Time: 15 min

Ingredients

- 2 (4 oz) boneless pork chops
- 1 tbsp honey
- 1 garlic clove (minced)
- 1/4 cup low-sodium soy sauce
- 1 tbsp olive oil

Instructions

1. Heat olive oil in a pan. Sear pork chops for 4 minutes per side.

2. Mix honey, soy sauce, and garlic. Pour over pork and cook for 5 minutes.

Nutritional Info (per serving)

Calories: 350 | Protein: 35g | Carbs: 15g | Fat: 12g | Fiber: 1g

VEGETABLE FRIED RICE

Smart Points: 5 | Servings: 2 | Prep Time: 10 min | Cook Time: 15 min

Ingredients

- 1 cup cooked brown rice
- 1/2 cup peas and carrots (frozen)
- 2 eggs (scrambled)
- 2 tbsp soy sauce

Instructions

1. Cook eggs in a pan. Remove and set aside.

2. Sauté vegetables for 3 minutes. Add rice, soy sauce, and eggs. Stir and serve.

Nutritional Info (per serving)

Calories: 280 | Protein: 10g | Carbs: 45g | Fat: 6g | Fiber: 4g

SPINACH AND FETA STUFFED CHICKEN BREAST

Smart Points: 4 | Servings: 2 | Prep Time: 10 min | Cook Time: 25 min

Ingredients

- 2 boneless, skinless chicken breasts (about 5 oz each)
- 1/2 cup fresh spinach (chopped)
- 1/4 cup crumbled feta cheese
- 1 garlic clove (minced)
- 1/4 tsp onion powder
- Salt and pepper (to taste)
- 1 tbsp olive oil

Instructions

1. Preheat oven to 375°F (190°C).

2. Slice a pocket into the side of each chicken breast, being careful not to cut all the way through.

3. In a small bowl, mix spinach, feta, garlic, onion powder, salt, and pepper. Stuff the mixture into the chicken pockets.

4. Heat olive oil in an oven-safe skillet and sear chicken for 2-3 minutes per side.

5. Transfer skillet to the oven and bake for 15-20 minutes, or until the internal temperature of the chicken reaches 165°F (74°C).

6. Let it rest for 5 minutes before serving.

Nutritional Info (per serving)

Calories: 280 | Protein: 35g | Carbs: 2g | Fat: 12g | Fiber: 1g

CHAPTER 5: VEGAN RECIPES

CHICKPEA AND SPINACH CURRY

Smart Points: 5 | Servings: 4 | Prep Time: 10 min | Cook Time: 25 min

Ingredients

- 1 (15 oz) can chickpeas (rinsed and drained)
- 1 cup fresh spinach (chopped)
- 1/2 cup coconut milk (light)
- 1 medium onion (chopped)
- 2 garlic cloves (minced)
- 1 tbsp olive oil
- 1 tsp curry powder
- 1/2 tsp turmeric powder
- 1/2 tsp cumin powder
- 1/2 tsp ground coriander
- 1/4 tsp red chili flakes (optional)
- Salt and pepper (to taste)

Instructions

1. Heat olive oil in a pan over medium heat. Sauté onions and garlic for 2-3 minutes.

2. Add curry powder, turmeric, cumin, coriander, and chili flakes. Stir for 1 minute.

3. Add chickpeas, coconut milk, and 1/2 cup water. Simmer for 10 minutes.

4. Add spinach and cook for another 5 minutes. Adjust salt and pepper.

5. Serve warm with rice or quinoa.

Nutritional Info (per serving)

Calories: 270 | Protein: 9g | Carbs: 32g | Fat: 12g | Fiber: 8g

TOFU AND VEGETABLE STIR-FRY

Smart Points: 6 | Servings: 2 | Prep Time: 15 min | Cook Time: 10 min

Ingredients

- 1/2 block extra-firm tofu (pressed and cubed)
- 1/2 cup broccoli florets
- 1/2 cup red bell pepper (sliced)
- 1/2 cup snap peas
- 2 garlic cloves (minced)
- 1 tbsp olive oil
- 2 tbsp low-sodium soy sauce
- 1 tbsp cornstarch (optional for thickening)
- 1/4 tsp red pepper flakes (optional)

Instructions

1. Heat olive oil in a large pan. Add tofu cubes and cook until golden (5-6 min). Remove from pan.

2. Add garlic, broccoli, red bell pepper, and snap peas. Sauté for 3-4 minutes.

3. Add tofu, soy sauce, and cornstarch (if using) to the pan. Stir and cook for 2-3 minutes.

4. Serve hot with brown rice or quinoa.

Nutritional Info (per serving)

Calories: 280 | Protein: 18g | Carbs: 20g | Fat: 14g | Fiber: 5g

VEGAN LENTIL TACOS

Smart Points: 4 | Servings: 4 | Prep Time: 10 min | Cook Time: 20 min

Ingredients

- 1 cup dry lentils (rinsed)
- 2 cups vegetable broth
- 1 tsp olive oil
- 1 small onion (chopped)
- 2 garlic cloves (minced)
- 1/2 tsp chili powder
- 1/2 tsp cumin
- 1/4 tsp smoked paprika
- 8 small corn tortillas

Instructions

1. Cook lentils in vegetable broth for 15-20 minutes.

2. Sauté onions and garlic in olive oil. Add cooked lentils, spices, salt, and pepper.

3. Warm tortillas and fill with lentil mixture. Top with lettuce, tomatoes, or avocado.

Nutritional Info (per serving)

Calories: 320 | Protein: 15g | Carbs: 48g | Fat: 6g | Fiber: 12g

SWEET POTATO AND BLACK BEAN CHILI

Smart Points: 5 | Servings: 4 | Prep Time: 10 min | Cook Time: 30 min

Ingredients

- 1 medium sweet potato (diced)
- 1 (15 oz) can black beans (rinsed)
- 1 onion (chopped)
- 2 garlic cloves (minced)
- 2 cups vegetable broth
- 1 (15 oz) can diced tomatoes
- 1/2 tsp cumin
- 1/2 tsp chili powder

Instructions

1. Sauté onion and garlic. Add sweet potato, black beans, tomatoes, and vegetable broth.

2. Stir in spices and simmer for 25-30 minutes.

3. Serve hot with cilantro garnish.

Nutritional Info (per serving)

Calories: 270 | Protein: 10g | Carbs: 50g | Fat: 3g | Fiber: 12g

VEGAN MUSHROOM STROGANOFF

Smart Points: 6 | Servings: 2 | Prep Time: 10 min | Cook Time: 20 min

Ingredients

- 8 oz whole wheat pasta
- 1 cup mushrooms (sliced)
- 1 small onion (chopped)
- 2 garlic cloves (minced)
- 1/2 cup unsweetened almond milk
- 1 tbsp cornstarch (for thickening)
- 1 tbsp olive oil

Instructions

1. Cook pasta according to package instructions.

2. Sauté mushrooms, onions, and garlic in olive oil for 5-6 minutes.

3. Mix almond milk with cornstarch. Pour into pan and cook until thick.

4. Combine with cooked pasta and serve.

Nutritional Info (per serving)

Calories: 350 | Protein: 12g | Carbs: 55g | Fat: 8g | Fiber: 9g

VEGAN BUDDHA BOWL

Smart Points: 7 | Servings: 1 | Prep Time: 10 min | Cook Time: 15 min

Ingredients

- 1/2 cup quinoa (cooked)
- 1/4 cup chickpeas (cooked)
- 1/4 cup shredded carrots
- 1/4 cup steamed broccoli
- 1/4 avocado (sliced)
- 1 tbsp tahini dressing

Instructions

1. Arrange quinoa, chickpeas, carrots, broccoli, and avocado in a bowl.

2. Drizzle with tahini dressing and serve.

Nutritional Info (per serving)

Calories: 400 | Protein: 15g | Carbs: 55g | Fat: 12g | Fiber: 10g

VEGAN BBQ JACKFRUIT SANDWICH

Smart Points: 6 | Servings: 2 | Prep Time: 10 min | Cook Time: 20 min

Ingredients

- 1 can jackfruit (drained)
- 1/4 cup BBQ sauce
- 2 whole wheat burger buns

Instructions

1. Sauté jackfruit with BBQ sauce for 15 minutes.

2. Serve on whole wheat buns with coleslaw.

Nutritional Info (per serving)

Calories: 310 | Protein: 10g | Carbs: 50g | Fat: 6g | Fiber: 8g

CHAPTER 6: DIABETES FRIENDLY RECIPES

TURKEY AND ZUCCHINI MEATBALLS

Smart Points: 3 | Servings: 4 | Prep Time: 15 min | Cook Time: 20 min

Ingredients

- 1 lb lean ground turkey
- 1/2 cup grated zucchini (squeezed to remove excess moisture)
- 1 garlic clove (minced)
- 1 egg
- 1/4 cup whole wheat breadcrumbs
- 1 tsp Italian seasoning
- Salt and pepper (to taste)
- 1 tbsp olive oil

Instructions

1. Preheat oven to 375°F (190°C).

2. In a bowl, mix turkey, zucchini, garlic, egg, breadcrumbs, Italian seasoning, salt, and pepper.

3. Shape mixture into small meatballs (about 1-inch in diameter).

4. Heat olive oil in a skillet and brown meatballs for 3-4 minutes.

5. Transfer to a baking sheet and bake for 15 minutes or until cooked through.

Nutritional Info (per serving)

Calories: 230 | Protein: 28g | Carbs: 7g | Fat: 10g | Fiber: 1g

Baked Chicken with Roasted Brussels Sprouts

Smart Points: 5 | Servings: 2 | Prep Time: 10 min | Cook Time: 25 min

Ingredients

- 2 (5 oz) boneless, skinless chicken breasts
- 1/2 lb Brussels sprouts (halved)
- 1 tbsp olive oil
- 1 tsp garlic powder
- Salt and pepper (to taste)

Instructions

1. Preheat oven to 400°F (204°C).

2. Place chicken breasts on one side of a baking sheet and Brussels sprouts on the other side.

3. Drizzle olive oil, garlic powder, salt, and pepper over both.

4. Bake for 20-25 minutes or until chicken reaches 165°F (74°C).

Nutritional Info (per serving)

Calories: 320 | Protein: 40g | Carbs: 10g | Fat: 12g | Fiber: 4g

BLACK BEAN AND QUINOA STUFFED BELL PEPPERS

Smart Points: 6 | Servings: 2 | Prep Time: 15 min | Cook Time: 30 min

Ingredients

- 2 large bell peppers (halved)
- 1/2 cup cooked quinoa
- 1/2 cup black beans (rinsed)
- 1/4 cup salsa
- 1/4 cup corn kernels
- 1/2 tsp cumin

Instructions

1. Preheat oven to 375°F (190°C).

2. Mix quinoa, black beans, salsa, corn, and cumin.

3. Stuff bell peppers with mixture. Bake for 25-30 minutes.

Nutritional Info (per serving)

Calories: 250 | Protein: 10g | Carbs: 40g | Fat: 4g | Fiber: 8g

LEMON GARLIC ROASTED CAULIFLOWER

Smart Points: 2 | Servings: 2 | Prep Time: 10 min | Cook Time: 20 min

Ingredients

- 1 head cauliflower (cut into florets)
- 1 lemon (juiced)
- 2 garlic cloves (minced)
- 1 tbsp olive oil

Instructions

1. Toss cauliflower in olive oil, lemon juice, and garlic.

2. Roast at 400°F (204°C) for 20-25 minutes.

Nutritional Info (per serving)

Calories: 150 | Protein: 5g | Carbs: 10g | Fat: 7g | Fiber: 3g

EGGPLANT STIR-FRY

Smart Points: 3 | Servings: 2 | Prep Time: 10 min | Cook Time: 15 min

Ingredients

- 1 medium eggplant (cubed)
- 1 tbsp low-sodium soy sauce
- 1 tbsp olive oil
- 1 garlic clove (minced)

Instructions

1. Sauté eggplant, garlic, and soy sauce in olive oil.

2. Cook for 10-12 minutes, stirring occasionally.

Nutritional Info (per serving)

Calories: 160 | Protein: 2g | Carbs: 14g | Fat: 9g | Fiber: 6g

VEGETABLE AND CHICKPEA SOUP

Smart Points: 3 | Servings: 2 | Prep Time: 10 min | Cook Time: 25 min

Ingredients

- 1/2 cup chickpeas (cooked)
- 1/2 cup carrots (chopped)
- 1/2 cup celery (chopped)

Instructions

Simmer veggies, chickpeas, and water for 25 minutes.

Nutritional Info (per serving)

Calories: 180 | Protein: 6g | Carbs: 30g | Fat: 2g | Fiber: 7g

GREEK CHICKPEA SALAD

Smart Points: 4 | Servings: 2 | Prep Time: 10 min

Ingredients

- 1/2 cup chickpeas
- 1/4 cup cucumbers (chopped)
- 1/4 cup tomatoes (chopped)

Instructions

Mix chickpeas, cucumbers, and tomatoes with lemon juice.

Nutritional Info (per serving)

Calories: 200 | Protein: 6g | Carbs: 30g | Fiber: 6g

CHAPTER 7: SMOOTHIES

STRAWBERRY BANANA BLISS SMOOTHIE

Smart Points: 4 per serving | Servings: 1 | Prep Time: 5 min

Ingredients

- 1/2 medium banana
- 1/2 cup fresh or frozen strawberries
- 1/2 cup unsweetened almond milk
- 1/4 cup non-fat Greek yogurt
- 1/2 tsp vanilla extract
- 1/2 cup ice

Instructions

1. Place all ingredients in a blender.
2. Blend on high for 1-2 minutes until smooth.
3. Pour into a glass and serve.

Nutritional Info (per serving)

Calories: 120 | Protein: 5g | Carbs: 22g | Fat: 2g | Fiber: 4g

TROPICAL GREEN DETOX SMOOTHIE

Smart Points: 3 | Servings: 1 | Prep Time: 5 min

Ingredients

- 1/2 cup fresh pineapple chunks
- 1/2 cup fresh spinach leaves
- 1/4 cup unsweetened coconut water
- 1/4 cup unsweetened almond milk
- 1/2 frozen banana
- 1/2 cup ice

Instructions

1. Add all ingredients to a blender.
2. Blend until smooth and creamy.
3. Serve immediately.

Nutritional Info (per serving)

Calories: 110 | Protein: 2g | Carbs: 25g | Fat: 1g | Fiber: 3g

BLUEBERRY ALMOND POWER SMOOTHIE

Smart Points: 5 | Servings: 1 | Prep Time: 5 min

Ingredients

- 1/2 cup fresh or frozen blueberries
- 1/2 cup unsweetened almond milk
- 1 tbsp almond butter (natural)
- 1/4 cup non-fat Greek yogurt
- 1/2 cup ice

Instructions

1. Blend all ingredients together in a blender.

2. Pour into a glass and enjoy!

Nutritional Info (per serving)

Calories: 160 | Protein: 6g | Carbs: 20g | Fat: 7g | Fiber: 4g

CHOCOLATE PEANUT BUTTER PROTEIN SMOOTHIE

Smart Points: 6 | Servings: 1 | Prep Time: 5 min

Ingredients

- 1 scoop chocolate protein powder
- 1/2 cup unsweetened almond milk
- 1 tbsp peanut butter (natural)
- 1/2 medium frozen banana
- 1/2 cup ice

Instructions

1. Add all ingredients to a blender.
2. Blend until smooth.
3. Pour and serve.

Nutritional Info (per serving)

Calories: 180 | Protein: 15g | Carbs: 24g | Fat: 7g | Fiber: 3g

MANGO COCONUT SMOOTHIE

Smart Points: 4 | Servings: 1 | Prep Time: 5 min

Ingredients

- 1/2 cup fresh or frozen mango chunks
- 1/4 cup unsweetened coconut water
- 1/4 cup unsweetened almond milk
- 1/2 frozen banana
- 1/2 cup ice

Instructions

1. Blend all ingredients together until smooth.

2. Serve and enjoy immediately.

Nutritional Info (per serving)

Calories: 130 | Protein: 2g | Carbs: 30g | Fat: 2g | Fiber: 3g

CREAMY AVOCADO BERRY SMOOTHIE

Smart Points: 6 | Servings: 1 | Prep Time: 5 min

Ingredients

- 1/4 avocado
- 1/2 cup frozen mixed berries
- 1/2 cup unsweetened almond milk
- 1/4 cup non-fat Greek yogurt
- 1/2 cup ice

Instructions

1. Blend all ingredients together until smooth.

2. Pour into a glass and enjoy.

Nutritional Info (per serving)

Calories: 150 | Protein: 5g | Carbs: 20g | Fat: 7g | Fiber: 4g

CINNAMON ROLL SMOOTHIE

Smart Points: 5 | Servings: 1 | Prep Time: 5 min

Ingredients

- 1/2 frozen banana
- 1/2 cup unsweetened almond milk
- 1/4 cup non-fat Greek yogurt
- 1/2 tsp ground cinnamon
- 1/2 tsp vanilla extract
- 1/2 cup ice

Instructions

1. Place all ingredients in a blender.
2. Blend on high until smooth and creamy.
3. Serve and enjoy.

Nutritional Info (per serving)

Calories: 130 | **Protein:** 5g | **Carbs:** 24g | **Fat:** 2g | **Fiber:** 3g

CARROT CAKE SMOOTHIE

Smart Points: 5 | Servings: 1 | Prep Time: 5 min

Ingredients

- 1/4 cup grated carrots
- 1/2 cup unsweetened almond milk
- 1/4 cup non-fat Greek yogurt
- 1/2 frozen banana
- 1/2 tsp ground cinnamon
- 1/4 tsp ground nutmeg
- 1/2 cup ice

Instructions

Blend all ingredients together until smooth.

Serve and enjoy.

Nutritional Info (per serving)

Calories: 130 | Protein: 5g | Carbs: 23g | Fat: 2g | Fiber: 3g

ORANGE CREAMSICLE SMOOTHIE

Smart Points: 4 | Servings: 1 | Prep Time: 5 min

Ingredients

- 1/2 cup fresh orange juice
- 1/4 cup unsweetened almond milk
- 1/4 cup non-fat Greek yogurt
- 1/2 frozen banana
- 1/2 cup ice

Instructions

1. Blend all ingredients together until smooth.
2. Serve immediately.

Nutritional Info (per serving)

Calories: 120 | Protein: 5g | Carbs: 25g | Fat: 1g | Fiber: 2g

APPLE PIE SMOOTHIE

Smart Points: 5 | Servings: 1 | Prep Time: 5 min

Ingredients

- 1/2 medium apple (chopped)
- 1/2 frozen banana
- 1/2 cup unsweetened almond milk
- 1/4 cup non-fat Greek yogurt
- 1/2 tsp ground cinnamon
- 1/2 tsp vanilla extract
- 1/2 cup ice

Instructions

1. Add all ingredients to a blender.
2. Blend until smooth and creamy.
3. Serve and enjoy.

Nutritional Info (per serving)

Calories: 140 | Protein: 5g | Carbs: 28g | Fat: 2g | Fiber: 3g

ENJOYING THIS BOOK?

SHARE YOUR FEEDBACK!

If you are enjoying the recipes, tips and insights in this book, or simply enjoyed flipping through the pages, I would greatly appreciate it if you could take a moment to leave your thoughts on Amazon.

Your feedback helps others discover this book and gives them confidence in starting their weight loss journey. Plus, hearing your thoughts inspires me to keep creating books that empower and excite you.

Leaving feedback on Amazon takes just a few minutes, but it makes a huge difference.

Thank you for your support and I wish you the best as you continue to flip through the pages of this book.

CRISPY AIR FRYER CHICKEN TENDERS

Smart Points: 5 | Servings: 2 | Prep Time: 10 min | Cook Time: 15 min

Ingredients

- 8 oz boneless, skinless chicken breast (cut into strips)
- 1/4 cup whole wheat panko breadcrumbs
- 1/4 cup grated Parmesan cheese
- 1 large egg (beaten)
- 1/2 tsp garlic powder
- 1/2 tsp onion powder
- 1/4 tsp smoked paprika
- Salt and pepper (to taste)

Instructions

1. Preheat air fryer to 375°F (190°C).

2. In a bowl, mix breadcrumbs, Parmesan, garlic powder, onion powder, paprika, salt, and pepper.

3. Dip each chicken strip into the egg, then coat with the breadcrumb mixture.

4. Place the coated chicken in a single layer in the air fryer basket.

5. Cook for 15 minutes, flipping halfway through.

6. Serve warm with a side of dipping sauce (optional).

Nutritional Info (per serving)

Calories: 250 | Protein: 30g | Carbs: 12g | Fat: 6g | Fiber: 2g

AIR FRYER GARLIC PARMESAN ZUCCHINI FRIES

Smart Points: 4 | Servings: 2 | Prep Time: 10 min | Cook Time: 12 min

Ingredients

- 2 medium zucchinis (cut into sticks)
- 1/4 cup whole wheat panko breadcrumbs
- 1/4 cup grated Parmesan cheese
- 1 large egg (beaten)
- 1/2 tsp garlic powder
- 1/4 tsp black pepper

Instructions

1. Preheat air fryer to 375°F (190°C).

2. Dip zucchini sticks into the beaten egg, then coat with breadcrumbs, Parmesan, garlic powder, and pepper.

3. Place zucchini sticks in a single layer in the air fryer basket.

4. Cook for 12 minutes, flipping halfway through.

5. Serve with a low-fat dipping sauce.

Nutritional Info (per serving)

Calories: 150 | Protein: 8g | Carbs: 14g | Fat: 6g | Fiber: 2g

AIR FRYER TURKEY MEATBALLS

Smart Points: 3 | Servings: 4 | Prep Time: 10 min | Cook Time: 12 min

Ingredients

- 1 lb lean ground turkey (93% lean)
- 1/4 cup whole wheat panko breadcrumbs
- 1 large egg
- 1/4 cup chopped onion
- 1 garlic clove (minced)
- 1/4 cup grated Parmesan cheese
- 1/2 tsp Italian seasoning

Instructions

1. Preheat air fryer to 380°F (193°C).

2. Mix all ingredients in a bowl and form into 12 small meatballs.

3. Place meatballs in the air fryer basket in a single layer.

4. Cook for 12 minutes, shaking the basket halfway through.

5. Serve with marinara sauce or over zucchini noodles.

Nutritional Info (per serving)

Calories: 180 | Protein: 20g | Carbs: 8g | Fat: 7g | Fiber: 1g

AIR FRYER BUFFALO CAULIFLOWER BITES

Smart Points: 2 | Servings: 4 | Prep Time: 10 min | Cook Time: 15 min

Ingredients

- 1 head cauliflower (cut into florets)
- 1/4 cup whole wheat flour
- 1/4 cup water
- 1/2 tsp garlic powder
- 1/2 cup buffalo sauce

Instructions

1. Preheat air fryer to 375°F (190°C).

2. Mix flour, water, and garlic powder to form a batter.

3. Dip cauliflower florets into the batter, shaking off excess.

4. Cook for 12-15 minutes, shaking halfway.

5. Toss cooked florets in buffalo sauce and serve.

Nutritional Info (per serving)

Calories: 100 | Protein: 3g | Carbs: 18g | Fat: 2g | Fiber: 4g

AIR FRYER CRISPY TOFU BITES

Smart Points: 3 | Servings: 2 | Prep Time: 10 min | Cook Time: 20 min

Ingredients

- 8 oz firm tofu (pressed and cubed)
- 1 tbsp low-sodium soy sauce
- 1 tbsp cornstarch
- 1/2 tsp garlic powder

Instructions

1. Toss tofu with soy sauce, garlic powder, and cornstarch.

2. Place tofu cubes in the air fryer basket.

3. Cook at 375°F (190°C) for 20 minutes, shaking halfway.

4. Serve with dipping sauce of choice.

Nutritional Info (per serving)

Calories: 150 | Protein: 12g | Carbs: 6g | Fat: 9g | Fiber: 2g

AIR FRYER SWEET POTATO FRIES

Smart Points: 4 | Servings: 2 | Prep Time: 10 min | Cook Time: 15 min

Ingredients

- 1 large sweet potato (cut into fries)
- 1 tbsp olive oil
- 1/2 tsp smoked paprika

Instructions

1. Toss sweet potatoes with olive oil and paprika.

2. Place in air fryer and cook at 375°F (190°C) for 15 minutes, shaking halfway.

3. Serve with ketchup or aioli.

Nutritional Info (per serving)

Calories: 160 | Protein: 2g | Carbs: 28g | Fat: 5g | Fiber: 4g

AIR FRYER GARLIC SHRIMP

Smart Points: 2 | Servings: 2 | Prep Time: 10 min | Cook Time: 8 min

Ingredients

- 1/2 lb shrimp (peeled and deveined)
- 1 tbsp olive oil
- 2 garlic cloves (minced)
- 1/2 tsp paprika

Instructions

1. Toss shrimp with olive oil, garlic, and paprika.

2. Place in air fryer at 375°F (190°C) for 8 minutes.

3. Serve with lemon wedges.

Nutritional Info (per serving)

Calories: 140 | Protein: 23g | Carbs: 1g | Fat: 5g | Fiber: 0g

Air Fryer Crispy Chickpeas

Smart Points: 2 | Servings: 4 | Prep Time: 5 min | Cook Time: 15 min

Ingredients

- 1 can chickpeas (rinsed, drained)
- 1 tbsp olive oil
- 1/2 tsp garlic powder

Instructions

1. Toss chickpeas with oil and garlic powder.

2. Place in air fryer at 400°F (204°C) for 15 minutes.

3. Shake basket halfway.

Nutritional Info (per serving)

Calories: 120 | Protein: 5g | Carbs: 15g | Fat: 4g | Fiber: 5g

Air Fryer Spiced Apple Chips

Smart Points: 1 | Servings: 2 | Prep Time: 5 min | Cook Time: 15 min

Ingredients

- 2 medium apples (sliced)
- 1/2 tsp ground cinnamon

Instructions

1. Toss apple slices with cinnamon.

2. Place in air fryer at 350°F (175°C) for 15 minutes.

Nutritional Info (per serving)

Calories: 95 | Protein: 0g | Carbs: 25g | Fiber: 3g

CHAPTER 9: SOUPS AND STEWS

CLASSIC VEGETABLE SOUP

Smart Points: 2 | Servings: 4 | Prep Time: 10 min | Cook Time: 25 min

Ingredients

- 1 tbsp olive oil
- 1 onion (chopped)
- 2 garlic cloves (minced)
- 2 carrots (sliced)
- 2 celery stalks (chopped)
- 1 zucchini (chopped)
- 1 cup green beans (cut into 1-inch pieces)
- 1 can (14 oz) diced tomatoes (no salt added)
- 4 cups low-sodium vegetable broth
- 1/2 tsp dried thyme
- 1/2 tsp Italian seasoning
- Salt and pepper (to taste)

Instructions

1. Heat olive oil in a large pot over medium heat. Add onion and garlic and sauté for 3 minutes.

2. Add carrots, celery, and zucchini, and cook for another 5 minutes.

3. Add green beans, diced tomatoes, vegetable broth, thyme, and Italian seasoning. Bring to a boil.

4. Reduce heat and simmer for 20 minutes, stirring occasionally.

5. Serve hot and enjoy.

Nutritional Info (per serving)

Calories: 120 | Protein: 3g | Carbs: 18g | Fat: 4g | Fiber: 5g

HEARTY LENTIL STEW

Smart Points: 4 | Servings: 4 | Prep Time: 10 min | Cook Time: 40 min

Ingredients

- 1 tbsp olive oil
- 1 onion (chopped)
- 2 carrots (chopped)
- 2 celery stalks (chopped)
- 3 garlic cloves (minced)
- 1 cup dry lentils (rinsed)
- 4 cups low-sodium vegetable broth
- 1 can (14 oz) diced tomatoes
- 1/2 tsp cumin
- 1/2 tsp paprika
- 1/4 tsp black pepper
- 1/2 tsp salt

Instructions

1. Heat olive oil in a pot. Add onion, garlic, carrots, and celery, cooking for 5 minutes.

2. Add lentils, broth, diced tomatoes, cumin, paprika, pepper, and salt. Bring to a boil.

3. Reduce heat and simmer for 35-40 minutes or until lentils are tender.

4. Serve hot with fresh herbs as a garnish.

Nutritional Info (per serving)

Calories: 180 | Protein: 10g | Carbs: 32g | Fat: 3g | Fiber: 11g

CHICKEN TORTILLA SOUP

Smart Points: 5 | Servings: 4 | Prep Time: 10 min | Cook Time: 30 min

Ingredients

- 1 lb boneless, skinless chicken breasts
- 1 tbsp olive oil
- 1 onion (chopped)
- 3 garlic cloves (minced)
- 1 green bell pepper (chopped)
- 1 can (14 oz) diced tomatoes
- 1 can (14 oz) black beans (rinsed)
- 4 cups low-sodium chicken broth
- 1 tsp cumin
- 1/2 tsp chili powder
- 1/2 tsp paprika
- Salt and pepper (to taste)
- 1/4 cup fresh cilantro (chopped)

Instructions

1. In a large pot, heat olive oil. Add onion, garlic, and bell pepper. Cook for 5 minutes.

2. Add chicken breasts, tomatoes, black beans, broth, cumin, chili powder, paprika, salt, and pepper. Bring to a boil.

3. Reduce heat, cover, and simmer for 25 minutes. Remove chicken, shred it, and return it to the pot.

4. Serve hot with fresh cilantro and optional tortilla chips.

Nutritional Info (per serving)

Calories: 210 | Protein: 25g | Carbs: 20g | Fat: 4g | Fiber: 7g

CREAMY CAULIFLOWER SOUP

Smart Points: 3 | Servings: 4 | Prep Time: 10 min | Cook Time: 20 min

Ingredients

- 1 head cauliflower (chopped)
- 1 onion (chopped)
- 3 garlic cloves (minced)
- 2 cups low-sodium vegetable broth
- 1 cup unsweetened almond milk
- 1/2 tsp garlic powder
- 1/2 tsp onion powder
- Salt and pepper (to taste)

Instructions

1. In a large pot, combine cauliflower, onion, garlic, and broth. Bring to a boil.

2. Reduce heat and simmer for 20 minutes.

3. Use an immersion blender to puree the soup until smooth.

4. Stir in almond milk, garlic powder, onion powder, salt, and pepper.

Nutritional Info (per serving)

Calories: 90 | Protein: 3g | Carbs: 12g | Fat: 2g | Fiber: 4g

BEEF AND BARLEY STEW

Smart Points: 6 | Servings: 4 | Prep Time: 15 min | Cook Time: 45 min

Ingredients

- 1/2 lb lean beef (cubed)
- 1 onion (chopped)
- 2 carrots (sliced)
- 2 garlic cloves (minced)
- 4 cups low-sodium beef broth
- 1/2 cup pearl barley
- 1/2 tsp dried thyme
- Salt and pepper (to taste)

Instructions

1. Brown beef in a large pot for 5-7 minutes.

2. Add onion, garlic, and carrots. Cook for 5 minutes.

3. Add beef broth, barley, thyme, salt, and pepper. Bring to a boil.

4. Reduce heat and simmer for 40 minutes.

Nutritional Info (per serving)

Calories: 250 | Protein: 20g | Carbs: 30g | Fat: 6g | Fiber: 6g

ITALIAN MINESTRONE SOUP

Smart Points: 4 | Servings: 4 | Prep Time: 10 min | Cook Time: 25 min

Ingredients

- 1 onion (chopped)
- 2 garlic cloves (minced)
- 2 carrots (chopped)
- 2 celery stalks (chopped)
- 1 zucchini (chopped)
- 1/2 cup elbow pasta (whole wheat)
- 4 cups low-sodium vegetable broth
- 1 can (14 oz) kidney beans (rinsed)
- 1 can (14 oz) diced tomatoes

Instructions

1. In a large pot, sauté onion, garlic, carrots, and celery for 5 minutes.

2. Add zucchini, pasta, broth, beans, and tomatoes. Bring to a boil.

3. Reduce heat and simmer for 20 minutes.

Nutritional Info (per serving)

Calories: 220 | Protein: 7g | Carbs: 40g | Fat: 2g | Fiber: 8g

BUTTERNUT SQUASH SOUP

Smart Points: 3 | Servings: 4 | Prep Time: 10 min | Cook Time: 20 min

Ingredients

- 1 tbsp olive oil
- 1 onion (chopped)
- 2 garlic cloves (minced)
- 1 large butternut squash (peeled and cubed)
- 3 cups low-sodium vegetable broth
- 1/2 tsp ground cinnamon
- 1/4 tsp ground nutmeg
- 1/4 cup unsweetened almond milk
- Salt and pepper (to taste)

Instructions

1. Heat olive oil in a large pot over medium heat. Add onion and garlic, sautéing for 3-4 minutes until fragrant.

2. Add cubed butternut squash, vegetable broth, cinnamon, nutmeg, salt, and pepper. Bring to a boil.

3. Reduce heat and simmer for 20 minutes, or until squash is tender.

4. Use an immersion blender to puree the soup until smooth.

5. Stir in the unsweetened almond milk. Adjust seasonings as needed.

6. Serve warm and garnish with a sprinkle of ground cinnamon or chopped fresh herbs (optional).

Nutritional Info (per serving)

Calories: 150 | Protein: 3g | Carbs: 29g | Fat: 3g | Fiber: 6g

CONCLUSION

By reaching this point in *The Weight Watchers Cookbook 2025,* you've already taken a significant step toward a healthier version of yourself. You might have gotten this book because you're ready to shed a few pounds, improve your overall well-being, or simply rediscover the joy of eating without guilt, this journey is yours to shape. And guess what? You've got everything you need right at your fingertips.

Think back to where you started. Maybe you were overwhelmed by the idea of meal planning or confused by the infamous Smart Points system. Now, you've gained the confidence to plan a week's worth of meals, navigate the grocery store like a pro, and even whip up satisfying breakfasts, lunches, and dinners that fuel your day while fitting into your plan.

You've learned the science behind the Weight Watchers program—why it works, how it reshapes your relationship with food, and why sustainability trumps crash diets every time. You've seen firsthand how small, consistent changes can lead to big, lasting results. And the best part? You've done it on your terms.

As you close this book, it's not the end. It's the beginning of a lifestyle you can build on. Maybe you start by tackling one new recipe each week or experimenting with different meal plans. Perhaps your goal is to master batch cooking or create your own version of the 7-day plan.

Set small, achievable goals that excite you. Don't forget that progress isn't about perfection, it is about consistency. When life gets busy (and it will), lean on the tips and tricks scattered throughout this book. Flip back to the grocery shopping guide, revisit your favorite smoothie recipe, and remind yourself why you started.

Weight loss and healthy living aren't linear paths. There will be days of triumph—when the scale moves, your clothes fit better, or you feel a surge of energy you haven't felt in years. There will also be days where motivation feels out of reach. That's normal. Use this book as your anchor. Let it remind you that one "off" day doesn't undo the weeks of progress you've already made.

Lean into your community. Join local Weight Watchers meetings, connect with others online, and celebrate small victories together. Surround yourself with people who understand your journey and will lift you up when you need it most.

You are capable of amazing things. Every healthy choice you make—whether it's swapping out sugary snacks for fruit, opting for water over soda, or preparing your own meals instead of ordering takeout—brings you closer to your goals.

Keep going. Keep experimenting. Keep enjoying food that not only nourishes your body but also brings joy to your table. The Weight Watchers lifestyle isn't about restriction; it's about balance, discovery, and ultimately, empowerment.

Thank you for letting this book be part of your journey. Now, go out there and make the next chapter of your life as vibrant and healthy as possible. You've got this!

Weekly Meal Planner

	BREAKFAST	LUNCH	DINNER	SNACKS
MON				
TUE				
WED				
THU				
FRI				
SAT				
SUN				

GROCERY LIST

_____
_____
_____
_____
_____
_____
_____
_____
_____
_____
_____
_____
_____
_____

NOTES

Weekly Meal Planner

	BREAKFAST	LUNCH	DINNER	SNACKS
MON				
TUE				
WED				
THU				
FRI				
SAT				
SUN				

GROCERY LIST

NOTES

Weekly Meal Planner

	BREAKFAST	LUNCH	DINNER	SNACKS
MON				
TUE				
WED				
THU				
FRI				
SAT				
SUN				

GROCERY LIST

NOTES

Weekly Meal Planner

	BREAKFAST	LUNCH	DINNER	SNACKS
MON				
TUE				
WED				
THU				
FRI				
SAT				
SUN				

GROCERY LIST

NOTES

Weekly Meal Planner

	BREAKFAST	LUNCH	DINNER	SNACKS
MON				
TUE				
WED				
THU				
FRI				
SAT				
SUN				

GROCERY LIST

NOTES

BONUS GIFT FOR YOU

As a thank you for purchasing **The Weight Watchers Cookbook 2025,** I've prepared an exclusive bonus to help you on your weight loss journey!

Scan the QR code below to access your free bonus — filled with **meal planning templates, 30 Days Meal Plan** and **helpful resources to keep you motivated and on track.**

Don't forget to leave feedback if you've enjoyed the recipes and tips in this book. It will make a huge difference in helping others discover this book.

And also, remember to check out my previous book, **'Quick and Easy Zero Point Weight Loss Cookbook'** packed with dishes only made from zero-point foods, here:

Printed in Great Britain
by Amazon